The Wealth Blueprint: Mastering the Art of Prosperity

Introduction

Welcome to "The Wealth Blueprint: Mastering the Art of Prosperity." In this comprehensive guide, we will embark on a transformative journey to unlock the secrets of financial success and empower you with the knowledge and tools to build lasting wealth. Designed specifically for readers in the British context, this book is your roadmap to navigate the ever-changing landscape of money earning and achieve true prosperity.

In today's world, financial security and abundance have become essential aspirations for individuals seeking freedom, opportunities, and a better quality of life. Whether you are just starting your financial journey or looking to enhance your existing wealth, "The Wealth Blueprint" offers practical insights, expert advice, and proven strategies to help you create a solid foundation for financial success.

Throughout this book, we will explore a wide range of topics, from income generation and investment strategies to effective money management and cultivating a wealth mindset. You will discover the principles and techniques employed by successful individuals who have mastered the art of prosperity and attained financial independence.

One of the key elements of this book is its focus on the British context. By understanding the unique opportunities and challenges present in the UK, you will be equipped with the necessary knowledge to make informed decisions and navigate the intricacies of the British financial landscape. From exploring investment opportunities in London's property market to understanding the nuances of tax regulations, "The Wealth Blueprint" provides insights specific to the UK that will help you make sound financial choices.

"The Wealth Blueprint" is not just a theoretical guide but a practical resource designed to empower you to take action. You will find actionable steps, real-life case studies, and valuable exercises that will allow you to apply the principles discussed and see tangible results in your financial journey.

It is important to remember that mastering the art of prosperity is a continuous process. As you progress through this book, you will gain not only financial knowledge but also a deeper understanding of your own values, beliefs, and aspirations. You will develop the skills and mindset necessary to adapt to changing economic landscapes, make informed financial decisions, and seize opportunities for growth.

Are you ready to embark on this transformative journey towards financial abundance and freedom? "The Wealth Blueprint: Mastering the Art of Prosperity" is here to guide you every step of the way. Together, let's unlock the secrets of wealth creation, cultivate a prosperous mindset, and build a solid financial future that aligns with your dreams and aspirations.

Index

Appendix: Resources for Further Exploration

- Recommended Books, Websites, and Podcasts
- Financial Tools and Apps for Money Management
- Professional Networks and Communities for Ongoing Support

Chapter 1: Understandig Your Financial Goals

Welcome to Chapter 1 of "The Wealth Blueprint: Mastering the Art of Prosperity." In this chapter, we will embark on a journey to discover and define your financial goals. Understanding your aspirations is crucial to creating a roadmap for achieving financial success. So, let's dive in and explore how you can identify both your long-term dreams and short-term objectives.

Section 1: Defining Your Long-Term Financial Aspirations

1.1 Creating a Vision for Your Financial Future:
To begin, take a moment to reflect on what financial abundance means to you. Close your eyes and envision your ideal lifestyle, career achievements, and personal goals. Consider aspects such as homeownership, retirement plans, travel, and philanthropy. Allow yourself to dream big and imagine the life you desire.

1.2 Setting S.M.A.R.T. Goals:
Now that you have an idea of your financial dreams, it's time to break them down into actionable goals. Introducing the concept of S.M.A.R.T. goals – Specific, Measurable, Achievable, Relevant, and Time-bound. By following these criteria, you can create goals that are clear, realistic, and aligned with your values and priorities.

For example, instead of setting a vague goal like "I want to be rich," a S.M.A.R.T. goal would be "I will accumulate £1 million in savings and investments within the next 15 years by consistently saving and investing 20% of my income."

Section 2: Defining Short-Term Objectives for Immediate Progress

2.1 Assessing Your Current Financial Situation:
To make progress towards your long-term goals, it's essential to understand your starting point. Take stock of your current financial situation by examining your income, expenses, assets, and liabilities. Create a comprehensive overview of your financial landscape, including bank statements, credit card balances, and investment accounts.

2.2 Prioritizing Short-Term Milestones:
With a clear understanding of your current situation, it's time to prioritize short-term milestones that will contribute to your long-term goals. Start by identifying areas where immediate progress is possible. These milestones should be specific, achievable within a reasonable timeframe, and aligned with your overall financial vision.

For instance, if you have high-interest debt, a short-term milestone could be to pay off your credit card balances within the next 12 months. If you plan to purchase a home, saving for a down payment could be another milestone. Evaluate each milestone's timeline and feasibility, considering factors such as your income, expenses, and any other financial commitments.

Section 3: Creating a Vision Board for Wealth and Success

3.1 The Power of Visualizing:
Visualization is a powerful tool for manifesting your financial goals. When you visualize your desired future, you activate your subconscious mind, which helps attract the necessary resources and opportunities. To harness this power, we'll create a vision board – a visual representation of your financial dreams and aspirations.

3.2 Curating Your Vision Board:
To create your vision board, gather images, words, and symbols that resonate with your financial aspirations. Look for pictures of your dream house, dream destinations, successful role models, and financial symbols like stacks of money or investment charts. Include affirmations and quotes that inspire and motivate you. You can create a physical vision board using a corkboard or poster, or create a digital version using online tools or apps.

Conclusion:
Congratulations on completing Chapter 1! You've taken the first steps towards understanding your financial goals. By defining your long-term aspirations, setting S.M.A.R.T. goals, assessing your current financial situation, prioritizing short-term milestones, and creating a vision board, you have set a strong foundation for your financial journey.

In the upcoming chapters, we will explore various income generation avenues, strategies to maximize your earning potential, and effective money management techniques. Together, we will help you master the art of prosperity and create a financially secure future. Keep the vision of your financial goals in mind as we continue this transformative journey.

Chapter 2: Exploring Income Generation Avenues

In Chapter 2 of "The Wealth Blueprint: Mastering the Art of Prosperity," we delve into the various avenues of income generation. While traditional employment provides a stable income for many, we will also explore entrepreneurship, passive income streams, and alternative sources of earning. By expanding your understanding of these avenues, you can maximize your earning potential and create multiple streams of income.

Section 1: Traditional Employment: Maximizing Your Earning Potential
In this section, we explore strategies to enhance your earning potential within the realm of traditional employment.
1.1 Evaluating Your Skills and Market Value:

- Assess your skills, qualifications, and experience to determine your market value.
- Research industry standards and salary benchmarks to ensure you are being compensated fairly.
- Identify areas where you can upskill or acquire additional certifications to increase your value in the job market.

1.2 Negotiation Techniques for Salary Increments and Job Offers:

- Learn effective negotiation strategies to secure higher salaries or better compensation packages.
- Understand the importance of demonstrating your value and highlighting your accomplishments during salary negotiations.
- Explore techniques such as anchoring, researching market rates, and emphasizing your unique skills and contributions.

Section 2: Entrepreneurship: Starting and Scaling Your Own Business Ventures

In this section, we delve into the world of entrepreneurship and explore how to start and scale your own business ventures.

2.1 Identifying Profitable Business Ideas:

- Explore methods for generating business ideas that align with your skills, passions, and market demand.
- Conduct market research to identify potential niches, target audiences, and competitive advantages.
- Evaluate the feasibility and profitability of your business ideas before committing resources.

2.2 Business Planning and Execution:

- Develop a comprehensive business plan that outlines your objectives, target market, marketing strategies, and financial projections.
- Understand the legal and regulatory requirements for setting up and operating a business in the UK.
- Implement effective project management techniques to ensure smooth execution and successful business operations.

Section 3: Passive Income Streams: Real Estate, Investments, and Royalties

In this section, we explore avenues for generating passive income that can provide ongoing financial benefits.

3.1 Real Estate Investments:

- Understand the potential benefits of real estate investments, such as rental properties, commercial spaces, or real estate investment trusts (REITs).
- Learn about property evaluation, financing options, property management, and the legal aspects of real estate investments.

3.2 Investments in Stocks, Bonds, and Mutual Funds:

- Familiarize yourself with investment options such as stocks, bonds, and mutual funds.
- Learn how to assess investment risks, diversify your portfolio, and make informed investment decisions.
- Explore the potential for capital appreciation, dividend income, and long-term wealth growth through investments.

3.3 Royalties and Intellectual Property:

- Discover how you can generate income from intellectual property, such as books, music, patents, or trademarks.
- Understand the process of copyrighting, licensing, and monetizing your intellectual creations.
- Explore opportunities for passive income through royalties, licensing agreements, or franchising.

Section 4: Alternative Income Sources: Freelancing, Gig Economy, and Digital Platforms
In this section, we explore alternative sources of income through freelancing, gig economy opportunities, and digital platforms.
4.1 Freelancing and Consulting:

- Learn how to leverage your skills and expertise to offer freelance services or consulting work.

- Understand how to market yourself, find clients, negotiate contracts, and establish a strong reputation in your chosen field.
- Explore digital platforms and freelance marketplaces that connect freelancers with potential clients.

4.2 Gig Economy and Sharing Economy:

- Explore opportunities in the gig economy, such as driving for ride-sharing services, delivering food, or providing on-demand services.
- Understand the benefits and challenges of working in the sharing economy and learn strategies to maximize your earnings.

4.3 Digital Platforms and Online Business:

- Discover the potential of online business ventures, such as e-commerce, affiliate marketing, or creating digital products.
- Learn about building an online presence, driving traffic to your website or online store, and utilizing social media for marketing purposes.

Conclusion:
In Chapter 2, we have explored a wide range of income generation avenues. By expanding your knowledge and understanding of traditional employment, entrepreneurship, passive income streams, and alternative sources of earning, you can take steps towards maximizing your earning potential. As you progress through the book, we will dive deeper into each avenue, providing practical strategies and insights to help you build multiple streams of income and achieve financial prosperity.

Chapter 3: Unleashing Your Earning Potential

In Chapter 3 of "The Wealth Blueprint: Mastering the Art of Prosperity," we focus on unleashing your earning potential. By expanding your skills, enhancing your market value, and capitalizing on emerging opportunities, you can take proactive steps to increase your income. This chapter explores various strategies and techniques that will empower you to maximize your earning capacity.

Section 1: Negotiation Techniques for Salary Increments and Job Offers
In this section, we delve into the art of negotiation, providing you with valuable techniques to secure higher salaries and better compensation packages.
1.1 Understanding Your Worth:

- Learn how to evaluate your skills, experience, and qualifications to determine your true value in the job market.
- Research industry benchmarks and salary ranges to gain insight into appropriate compensation levels.
- Understand the importance of aligning your salary expectations with your market value.

1.2 Preparing for Negotiation:

- Develop a strategic approach to negotiation by setting clear objectives and defining your desired outcomes.
- Gather relevant data and evidence to support your case, such as examples of your achievements, industry trends, and market rates.

- Anticipate potential objections or counterarguments and prepare responses to overcome them effectively.

1.3 Effective Negotiation Techniques:

- Learn essential negotiation skills, including active listening, effective communication, and building rapport with the other party.
- Explore techniques such as anchoring, framing, and creating mutually beneficial agreements.
- Understand the importance of non-monetary benefits and perks in negotiating a comprehensive compensation package.

Section 2: Enhancing Your Market Value through Professional Development and Education
In this section, we explore how continuous learning and professional development can boost your market value and open doors to higher income opportunities.
2.1 Identifying Skill Gaps and Target Areas for Improvement:

- Assess your current skill set and identify areas where you can enhance your knowledge or acquire new skills.
- Research industry trends, emerging technologies, and in-demand skills to align your professional development efforts with market demands.
- Explore both formal education programs and self-study options to expand your knowledge base.

2.2 Investing in Education and Training:

- Evaluate different educational pathways, such as degree programs, certifications, workshops, or online courses.

- Consider the return on investment (ROI) of each educational opportunity in terms of career advancement and increased earning potential.
- Explore funding options, scholarships, or employer-sponsored programs to support your educational endeavors.

2.3 Showcasing Your Skills and Expertise:

- Develop a personal brand that highlights your unique skills, accomplishments, and expertise.
- Leverage online platforms and professional networks to showcase your portfolio, receive endorsements, and attract potential employers or clients.
- Engage in thought leadership activities, such as writing articles, speaking at conferences, or participating in industry forums, to establish yourself as an authority in your field.

Section 3: Exploring Side Hustles and Monetizing Your Skills and Hobbies

In this section, we explore the concept of side hustles and how you can monetize your skills, talents, and hobbies to generate additional income.

3.1 Identifying Profitable Side Hustle Opportunities:

- Assess your skills, talents, and hobbies to identify potential side hustle opportunities that align with your interests and strengths.
- Research market demand, competition, and profitability to ensure the viability of your chosen side hustle.
- Consider the scalability and flexibility of different side hustle options to find the best fit for your lifestyle and goals.

3.2 Building a Side Hustle Business:

- Develop a strategic plan for launching and growing your side hustle business, including target audience identification, marketing strategies, and financial projections.
- Utilize online platforms, social media, and digital marketing techniques to reach your target market and promote your side hustle.
- Implement effective time management strategies to balance your side hustle with your primary job or other commitments.

3.3 Monetizing Your Skills and Expertise:

- Explore opportunities to monetize your skills and expertise through consulting, coaching, or freelance work.
- Leverage online marketplaces, freelancing platforms, and professional networks to find clients and projects that align with your skills.
- Establish a strong reputation for delivering high-quality work and exceeding client expectations to attract repeat business and referrals.

Conclusion:
Chapter 3 has provided valuable insights and strategies to unleash your earning potential. By mastering negotiation techniques, enhancing your market value through continuous learning, and exploring side hustles and monetizing your skills, you can create multiple avenues for increasing your income. As you implement these strategies, you will be one step closer to achieving your financial goals and building lasting wealth.

Chapter 4: Mastering Money Management

In Chapter 4 of "The Wealth Blueprint: Mastering the Art of Prosperity," we shift our focus to the crucial aspect of money management. Effective money management is the foundation of financial success and wealth creation. In this chapter, we will explore strategies for budgeting, reducing debt, increasing savings, building an emergency fund, and making informed investment decisions. By mastering the art of money management, you will gain control over your finances and pave the way for long-term prosperity.

Section 1: The Power of Budgeting and Tracking Expenses
In this section, we emphasize the importance of budgeting and tracking your expenses to gain a clear understanding of your financial situation.
1.1 Creating a Personalized Budget:

- Learn how to create a budget that aligns with your financial goals and priorities.
- Identify your income sources, fixed expenses, variable expenses, and financial obligations.
- Allocate funds for savings, investments, and discretionary spending.

1.2 Tracking and Analyzing Expenses:

- Implement effective systems and tools to track your expenses on a regular basis.
- Categorize your expenses and analyze spending patterns to identify areas for improvement.

- Utilize budgeting apps or spreadsheets to automate expense tracking and gain real-time insights into your financial habits.

1.3 Adjusting and Fine-Tuning Your Budget:

- Regularly review and evaluate your budget to ensure it remains aligned with your financial goals and lifestyle.
- Make necessary adjustments to accommodate changes in income, expenses, or financial priorities.
- Seek opportunities to reduce unnecessary expenses and redirect funds towards savings or investments.

Section 2: Strategies for Reducing Debt and Increasing Savings
In this section, we explore strategies to reduce debt burdens and increase your savings, laying the groundwork for financial stability and future wealth.
2.1 Managing and Consolidating Debt:

- Understand different types of debt and their impact on your financial well-being.
- Implement debt management techniques such as snowball or avalanche methods to prioritize and pay off debts.
- Explore debt consolidation options to simplify repayment and potentially lower interest rates.

2.2 Building an Effective Savings Plan:

- Set savings goals and establish a systematic approach to saving money.
- Explore different savings vehicles such as savings accounts, fixed deposits, or individual savings accounts (ISAs).

- Automate savings contributions to ensure consistency and discipline in building your savings.

2.3 Cultivating Healthy Spending Habits:

- Develop mindful spending habits by distinguishing between needs and wants.
- Implement strategies such as the 24-hour rule or the 50/30/20 rule to curb impulsive spending and prioritize savings.
- Seek alternative ways to enjoy experiences or purchase items without compromising your long-term financial goals.

Section 3: Building an Emergency Fund and Protecting Your Financial Well-Being
In this section, we explore the importance of building an emergency fund and protecting yourself against unforeseen financial challenges.
3.1 Understanding the Importance of an Emergency Fund:

- Learn why having an emergency fund is essential for financial security and peace of mind.
- Determine the ideal amount for your emergency fund, typically three to six months' worth of living expenses.
- Explore options for keeping your emergency fund easily accessible while earning some interest.

3.2 Mitigating Financial Risks with Insurance:

- Assess your insurance needs and obtain coverage for areas such as health, life, disability, property, or liability.
- Understand the terms, coverage limits, and deductibles of your insurance policies.

- Regularly review and update your insurance coverage to ensure it aligns with your evolving circumstances.

Section 4: Understanding the Role of Investments in Wealth Preservation

In this section, we delve into the world of investments and explore how they contribute to long-term wealth preservation and growth.

4.1 Investment Basics and Risk Assessment:

- Understand fundamental investment concepts, such as risk, return, diversification, and asset allocation.
- Assess your risk tolerance and investment goals to determine an appropriate investment strategy.
- Seek professional advice or educate yourself on different investment options and their associated risks.

4.2 Exploring Investment Vehicles:

- Explore a range of investment options, including stocks, bonds, mutual funds, index funds, real estate, or retirement accounts.
- Consider factors such as liquidity, potential returns, tax implications, and investment time horizon when selecting investment vehicles.
- Create a well-diversified investment portfolio that aligns with your risk tolerance and financial objectives.

4.3 Monitoring and Adjusting Your Investment Portfolio:

- Regularly review and assess the performance of your investment portfolio.
- Rebalance your portfolio periodically to maintain desired asset allocations and adjust to changing market conditions.

- Stay informed about economic trends, market news, and regulatory changes that may impact your investment decisions.

Conclusion:
Chapter 4 has provided valuable insights and strategies for mastering money management. By creating a budget, reducing debt, increasing savings, building an emergency fund, and making informed investment decisions, you can take control of your financial future. Implementing these strategies will enable you to lay a solid foundation for wealth creation and long-term financial well-being.

Chapter 5: The Mindset of Wealth Creation

In Chapter 5 of "The Wealth Blueprint: Mastering the Art of Prosperity," we delve into the mindset of wealth creation. While financial strategies and tactics are essential, developing the right mindset is equally important for long-term success. This chapter explores the beliefs, attitudes, and habits that empower individuals to create and sustain wealth. By adopting a wealth-oriented mindset, you can overcome obstacles, embrace opportunities, and manifest abundance in your financial journey.

Section 1: Cultivating a Positive Money Mindset
In this section, we focus on cultivating a positive and abundance-oriented mindset that lays the foundation for wealth creation.
1.1 Shifting from Scarcity to Abundance:

- Identify and challenge limiting beliefs and scarcity mentality that hinder your financial progress.
- Embrace an abundance mindset by focusing on opportunities, gratitude, and the belief that wealth is attainable.
- Surround yourself with positive influences and affirmations that reinforce your wealth-oriented mindset.

1.2 Developing Self-Worth and Money Mindset Alignment:

- Recognize your inherent value and worth beyond your financial status or possessions.
- Align your money mindset with your personal values, goals, and aspirations.

- Embrace a healthy relationship with money, understanding that it is a tool for creating opportunities and improving lives.

1.3 Practicing Gratitude and Financial Mindfulness:

- Cultivate a daily gratitude practice to appreciate the abundance in your life, both financial and non-financial.
- Practice financial mindfulness by being aware of your spending habits, making conscious financial decisions, and regularly reviewing your financial goals.

Section 2: Overcoming Limiting Beliefs and Financial Roadblocks

In this section, we address common limiting beliefs and financial roadblocks that can hinder wealth creation and provide strategies for overcoming them.

2.1 Identifying and Challenging Limiting Beliefs:

- Identify and confront self-limiting beliefs related to money, success, and wealth.
- Challenge these beliefs by gathering evidence to the contrary, seeking alternative perspectives, and reframing negative thoughts.
- Embrace empowering beliefs that support your financial growth and abundance.

2.2 Overcoming Fear and Taking Calculated Risks:

- Understand the role of fear in financial decision-making and how it can hold you back from pursuing wealth-building opportunities.
- Develop strategies to manage and mitigate fear, such as conducting thorough research, seeking advice from experts, and taking calculated risks.

- Embrace a growth mindset that views failures as learning experiences and stepping stones towards success.

2.3 Building Resilience and Persistence:

- Recognize that setbacks and challenges are inevitable on the path to wealth creation.
- Build resilience by cultivating a positive mindset, maintaining a strong support system, and developing coping strategies.
- Cultivate persistence and a willingness to adapt, pivot, and persevere in the face of obstacles.

Section 3: Embracing a Wealth-Building Lifestyle

In this section, we explore the habits, behaviors, and lifestyle choices that support a wealth-building mindset and pave the way for sustained prosperity.

3.1 Financial Goal Setting and Visualization:

- Set clear and specific financial goals that align with your vision of wealth and success.
- Utilize visualization techniques to imagine and embody your future financial abundance.
- Break down your goals into actionable steps and create a plan to achieve them.

3.2 Continuous Learning and Personal Development:

- Embrace a lifelong learning mindset and invest in personal development.
- Stay updated with industry trends, financial knowledge, and emerging opportunities.

- Seek out mentors, attend seminars, read books, and engage in networking activities to expand your knowledge and professional network.

3.3 Surrounding Yourself with a Wealth-Building Network:

- Surround yourself with like-minded individuals who share your financial aspirations.
- Cultivate relationships with mentors, successful individuals, and supportive peers who can provide guidance, inspiration, and accountability.
- Participate in communities, mastermind groups, or online forums focused on wealth creation.

Conclusion:
Chapter 5 has explored the mindset of wealth creation, emphasizing the importance of cultivating a positive money mindset, overcoming limiting beliefs, and embracing a wealth-building lifestyle. By adopting these principles and integrating them into your daily life, you can transform your relationship with money, embrace abundance, and manifest lasting financial prosperity.

Chapter 6: Building Generational Wealth

In Chapter 6 of "The Wealth Blueprint: Mastering the Art of Prosperity," we shift our focus to the concept of building generational wealth. Generational wealth refers to the accumulation of assets, investments, and financial resources that can be passed down from one generation to another. This chapter explores strategies and considerations for creating a legacy of wealth that can benefit not only your immediate family but also future generations.

Section 1: Understanding the Importance of Generational Wealth
In this section, we delve into the significance of generational wealth and its potential impact on the financial well-being of your family lineage.
1.1 The Benefits of Generational Wealth:

- Explore the advantages that generational wealth can bring, including financial security, opportunities for education, entrepreneurship, philanthropy, and intergenerational financial support.
- Understand how generational wealth can break cycles of poverty and create a platform for future generations to thrive.

1.2 Recognizing the Responsibility of Wealth Stewardship:

- Embrace the responsibility of being a steward of wealth and ensuring its preservation and growth for future generations.
- Understand the impact of financial decisions and behaviors on the long-term sustainability of generational wealth.

- Emphasize the values of financial education, responsible wealth management, and the cultivation of a wealth-building mindset within your family.

Section 2: Estate Planning and Wealth Transfer Strategies
In this section, we explore estate planning and wealth transfer strategies that facilitate the smooth transfer of assets and resources across generations.
2.1 Creating an Estate Plan:

- Understand the importance of estate planning and the various components involved, such as wills, trusts, and power of attorney.
- Seek professional guidance from estate planning attorneys or financial advisors to develop a comprehensive estate plan tailored to your specific needs and goals.
- Consider factors such as tax implications, asset protection, and family dynamics when structuring your estate plan.

2.2 Implementing Wealth Transfer Strategies:

- Explore different wealth transfer strategies, such as gifting, trusts, charitable foundations, or family partnerships.
- Determine the most suitable strategy for your circumstances, considering factors such as asset types, tax implications, and the desired level of control or flexibility.
- Engage in open and transparent communication with your family members to ensure they understand your intentions and plans for wealth transfer.

Section 3: Educating and Empowering Future Generations

In this section, we discuss the importance of financial education and empowerment for future generations to sustain and grow generational wealth.

3.1 Instilling Financial Literacy:

- Introduce financial education to your children and grandchildren from an early age.
- Teach them the principles of budgeting, saving, investing, and responsible money management.
- Encourage them to develop a wealth-building mindset and provide opportunities for them to practice financial decision-making.

3.2 Mentoring and Passing Down Financial Wisdom:

- Share your financial experiences, successes, and lessons learned with future generations.
- Act as a mentor and guide, providing guidance and support as they navigate their own financial journeys.
- Encourage them to seek education, pursue their passions, and make informed financial decisions that align with their values and goals.

3.3 Fostering an Entrepreneurial Spirit:

- Encourage entrepreneurship within your family by supporting and nurturing business ideas and ventures.
- Provide resources, mentorship, and networking opportunities to help them succeed in their entrepreneurial pursuits.
- Emphasize the importance of innovation, adaptability, and long-term wealth-building strategies in their entrepreneurial endeavors.

Conclusion:

Chapter 6 has explored the concept of building generational wealth, emphasizing the importance of responsible wealth stewardship, estate planning, and financial education for future generations. By implementing these strategies and instilling a mindset of financial empowerment, you can create a lasting legacy of wealth that benefits not only your immediate family but also future generations.

Chapter 7: Navigating Economic Challenges and Market Volatility

Chapter 7 of "The Wealth Blueprint: Mastering the Art of Prosperity" addresses the inevitable economic challenges and market volatility that individuals may face on their journey towards financial success. In this chapter, we explore strategies for navigating economic downturns, managing financial risks, and making informed decisions to protect and grow your wealth amidst changing market conditions.

Section 1: Understanding Economic Cycles and Downturns
In this section, we provide an overview of economic cycles and the potential impact of downturns on personal finances.
1.1 Economic Cycles and their Phases:

- Understand the different phases of economic cycles, including expansion, peak, contraction, and trough.
- Recognize the indicators and signals that indicate shifts in the economic landscape.
- Learn how economic cycles can affect employment, investments, and overall financial well-being.

1.2 Anticipating and Preparing for Economic Downturns:

- Develop strategies to anticipate economic downturns by monitoring economic indicators and staying informed about market trends.
- Prepare a contingency plan to safeguard your finances in the event of a downturn, including building an emergency fund and diversifying your investments.

- Seek professional advice from financial advisors or wealth managers who can provide guidance on navigating economic challenges.

Section 2: Risk Management Strategies
In this section, we delve into risk management strategies that help protect your wealth during times of market volatility.
2.1 Diversification and Asset Allocation:

- Understand the importance of diversifying your investment portfolio across different asset classes and industries.
- Explore asset allocation strategies that align with your risk tolerance and financial goals.
- Regularly review and rebalance your portfolio to maintain desired asset allocations and mitigate risks.

2.2 Hedging and Insurance:

- Consider hedging strategies, such as purchasing options or futures contracts, to protect against potential losses in specific investments or market segments.
- Evaluate your insurance coverage and ensure it adequately protects your assets, liabilities, and financial interests.
- Work with insurance professionals to identify potential gaps in coverage and make necessary adjustments.

Section 3: Making Informed Investment Decisions
In this section, we focus on making informed investment decisions amidst market volatility and economic uncertainties.
3.1 Conducting Thorough Research and Due Diligence:

- Conduct comprehensive research on investment opportunities, including analyzing financial statements, evaluating market trends, and understanding industry dynamics.
- Seek professional advice or collaborate with financial advisors who can provide expertise and insights.
- Avoid making impulsive investment decisions based on short-term market fluctuations.

3.2 Embracing a Long-Term Investment Approach:

- Adopt a long-term investment perspective that focuses on your financial goals and investment time horizon.
- Resist the urge to react emotionally to market volatility and instead maintain a disciplined investment strategy.
- Stay informed about economic developments and market trends but avoid excessive monitoring or overtrading.

3.3 Investment Education and Continuous Learning:

- Invest in your own financial education to enhance your understanding of investment principles and strategies.
- Attend seminars, workshops, or webinars to expand your knowledge and stay updated on investment trends.
- Engage in discussions and networking with experienced investors to gain valuable insights and perspectives.

Section 4: Maintaining Resilience and Adaptability
In this section, we discuss the importance of maintaining resilience and adaptability during economic challenges.
4.1 Cultivating Emotional Intelligence:

- Develop emotional intelligence to manage stress, anxiety, and fear associated with market volatility.
- Practice mindfulness, meditation, or other stress management techniques to maintain emotional well-being.
- Seek support from family, friends, or professionals when needed.

4.2 Capitalizing on Opportunities:

- Recognize that economic challenges and market downturns can present opportunities for wealth creation.
- Maintain a keen eye for undervalued investments or sectors poised for recovery.
- Be prepared to capitalize on opportunities when they arise, balancing calculated risk-taking with prudent decision-making.

Conclusion:
Chapter 7 has provided valuable insights and strategies for navigating economic challenges and market volatility. By understanding economic cycles, implementing risk management strategies, making informed investment decisions, and maintaining resilience, you can protect and grow your wealth even in the face of uncertainty.

www.ingramcontent.com/pod-product-compliance
Lightning Source LLC
Chambersburg PA
CBHW070909220526
45466CB00005B/2183